IT'S TIME TO EAT
LYCHEE FRUIT

It's Time to Eat LYCHEE FRUIT

Walter the Educator

Silent King Books
A WhichHead Entertainment Imprint

Copyright © 2024 by Walter the Educator

All rights reserved. No part of this book may be reproduced in any manner whatsoever without written per- mission except in the case of brief quotations embodied in critical articles and reviews.

First Printing, 2024

Disclaimer

This book is a literary work; the story is not about specific persons, locations, situations, and/or circumstances unless mentioned in a historical context. Any resemblance to real persons, locations, situations, and/or circumstances is coincidental. This book is for entertainment and informational purposes only. The author and publisher offer this information without warranties expressed or implied. No matter the grounds, neither the author nor the publisher will be accountable for any losses, injuries, or other damages caused by the reader's use of this book. The use of this book acknowledges an understanding and acceptance of this disclaimer.

It's Time to Eat LYCHEE FRUIT is a collectible early learning book by Walter the Educator suitable for all ages belonging to Walter the Educator's Time to Eat Book Series. Collect more books at WaltertheEducator.com

USE THE EXTRA SPACE TO TAKE NOTES AND DOCUMENT YOUR MEMORIES

LYCHEE FRUIT

It's time to eat, come gather 'round,

It's Time to Eat
Lychee Fruit

Lychee fruit is where joy is found!

Red and bumpy, small and sweet,

A perfect snack for hands and feet.

Pick it fresh, or buy a bunch,

Lychee fruit is great to munch.

The outside's rough, the inside's white,

A juicy treasure, pure delight!

Peel the skin, just like a coat,

A tasty fruit will make you float.

Round and shiny, soft and fair,

Its sweet perfume fills up the air.

Take a nibble, take a bite,

Lychee fruit feels just so right.

It's sweet as honey, soft as cream,

A fruity treat, a lovely dream!

It's Time to Eat
Lychee Fruit

Inside the fruit, a seed you'll find,

It's smooth and dark, one of a kind.

Don't eat the seed, just set it down,

The fruit's the star, its taste will crown!

Share with friends, share with all,

Lychee love is big, not small.

With every bite, you'll feel so bright,

This fruit's pure magic, day or night.

It grows on trees, so tall and green,

A lovely sight, a fruity scene.

In summer sun, it's ripe and true,

Lychee fruit is made for you!

You can eat it fresh or make a juice,

Its flavor's great for any use.

From ice cream bowls to jellies sweet,

It's Time to Eat Lychee Fruit

Lychee treats are such a feat!

So grab some lychee, have a taste,

Don't let this moment go to waste.

Its yummy flavor's hard to beat,

Lychee fruit is fun to eat!

With every bite, you'll laugh and cheer,

Lychee fruit brings joy so near.

A special snack for me and you,

It's Time to Eat
Lychee Fruit

Time to eat, enjoy it too!

ABOUT THE CREATOR

Walter the Educator is one of the pseudonyms for Walter Anderson. Formally educated in Chemistry, Business, and Education, he is an educator, an author, a diverse entrepreneur, and he is the son of a disabled war veteran. "Walter the Educator" shares his time between educating and creating. He holds interests and owns several creative projects that entertain, enlighten, enhance, and educate, hoping to inspire and motivate you. Follow, find new works, and stay up to date with Walter the Educator™

at WaltertheEducator.com

www.ingramcontent.com/pod-product-compliance
Lightning Source LLC
LaVergne TN
LVHW052013060526
838201LV00059B/4007